PIANO · VOCAL · GUITAR

MARIAH CAREY · MUSIC BOX

ISBN: 0-7935-2986-7

HAL Hal Leonard Publishing Corporation
7777 West Bluemound Road P.O. Box 13819 Milwaukee, WI 53213

All I've Ever Wanted

Words and Music by MARIAH CAREY
and WALTER AFANASIEFF

ANYTIME YOU NEED A FRIEND

Words and Music by MARIAH CAREY
and WALTER AFANASIEFF

Moderate ballad

If you're lone - ly
When the sha - dows

and need a friend
are clos - ing in

and trou - bles seem_ like
and your spir - it

they nev - er end,_____
dim - in - ish - ing,_____

just re - mem - ber
just re - mem - ber

to keep the faith _____
you're not a - lone _____

DREAMLOVER

Words and Music by MARIAH CAREY
and DAVE HALL

HERO

Words and Music by MARIAH CAREY
and WALTER AFANASIEFF

I'LL NEVER FORGET YOU

Words and Music by MARIAH CAREY
and BABYFACE

I'VE BEEN THINKING ABOUT YOU

Words and Music by MARIAH CAREY,
DAVID COLE and ROBERT CLIVILLES

JUST TO HOLD YOU ONCE AGAIN

Words and Music by MARIAH CAREY
and WALTER AFANASIEFF

MUSIC BOX

Words and Music by MARIAH CAREY
and WALTER AFANASIEFF

NOW THAT I KNOW

Words and Music by MARIAH CAREY,
DAVID COLE and ROBERT CLIVILLES

WITHOUT YOU

Words and Music by WILLIAM HAM
and TOM EVANS

Slow rock

Lyrics:

No, I can't for-get this eve-ning or your face as you were leav-ing, but I guess that's just the way the sto-ry goes. You al-ways smile but in your eyes your sor-row shows. Yes, it